Involving your workforce in health and safety

Good practice for all workplaces

HSE

Health and Safety
Executive

HSE Books

© Crown copyright 2008

First published 2008

ISBN 978 0 7176 6227 2

This guidance is issued by the Health and Safety Executive.
Following the guidance is not compulsory and you are
free to take other action. But if you do follow the guidance
you will normally be doing enough to comply with the law.
Health and safety inspectors seek to secure compliance with
the law and may refer to this guidance as illustrating good
practice.

Contents

Foreword

Chair of HSE

The world of work is continually changing, and poses new challenges in preventing and reducing accidents and ill health in the workplace. What remain constant are the essential principles of effective health and safety management, particularly good workforce involvement and strong and active leadership from the top.

Evidence shows that businesses with good workforce involvement in health and safety perform better in health and safety measures, and also tend to have better productivity and higher levels of workforce motivation. Like strong leadership, employee engagement is essential because everyone, from the most senior managers to individual employees, has a part to play in building a strong health and safety culture.

This new good practice guide on workforce involvement and consultation draws upon the established legislation, and by reflecting the range of workforce structures and arrangements which exist in workplaces today, captures the core of good workforce involvement.

It is built on the principles of trust, respect, co-operation and joint problem solving between employers and employees. These principles are vital because to reap the real benefits there has to be more than consultation; there has to be genuine employee participation in the decision-making process.

Judith Hackitt

Chair of the Arbitration and Conciliation Service (Acas)

When you read or hear about what makes an effective workplace the same ideas crop up again and again: engagement; involvement; trust; co-operation. All these ideas are based upon the same principle – employers and employees make better decisions together.

Acas has been working with businesses of all kinds and from all sectors for over thirty years. Our experience tells us that employee involvement really does make a difference – whether you are discussing job design, performance management, disciplinary procedures or health and safety. Research has shown that having an element of control over the way you do your job makes you feel more committed to an organisation. This commitment often makes an organisation more productive and successful.

Acas has recently published a guide *Health, work and wellbeing* (see www.acas.org.uk). We have identified six key indicators of a healthy workplace. One of these indicators describes an organisation where 'employees feel valued and involved'.

I am sure that this practical guide from HSE will help to promote workplaces that are safe and healthy on every level. By actively consulting and involving employees, co-operative working based on trust and openness can become a reality for the majority of workplaces in the UK.

Ed Sweeney

BOOK ORDER

COLEG SIR GAR 18170.001-001

Supplier	Dawson Books (UK)	Order Ref	PI/11/09/100
Order Date	18/06/2009	Item Ref	01
Quantity	1	ISBN	9780717662272
Unit Price	10.95	Currency	GBP
Instructions			

Author   HEALTH AND SAFETY EX
Title   INVOLVING YOUR WORKFORCE IN HEALTH AND SAFETY

Volume	HEALTH & SAFETY	Edition	
Format		Publisher	HEALTH AND SAFETY EXECUTIVE,
Shelf Mark			
Site			
Fund			
Sequence			
Loan Type			
Quantity	1		

How to use this guide

This guide gives you good practice advice on how to consult and involve your employees and their representatives on health and safety matters at work. It complements the Legal series publication L146 *Consulting workers on health and safety. Safety Representatives and Safety Committees Regulations 1977 (as amended) and Health and Safety (Consultation with Employees) Regulations 1996 (as amended). Approved Codes of Practice and guidance.*[1]

The guide is primarily aimed at medium to large employers. It will help them in their duty to consult and involve their employees on health and safety matters. It is advisable to include contracted, agency and temporary workers as well as direct employees in your consultation arrangements. Small businesses may find the good practice advice helpful, particularly the case studies. A free leaflet is also available from HSE which covers what employers need to know: *Consulting employees on health and safety: A brief guide to the law* (INDG232(rev1))[2] and there is also advice on HSE's website at: www.hse.gov.uk/involvement.

Employees, their health and safety representatives and trade unions may also find the guide useful as they are the people you will need to involve in the process, but it is your legal duty as the employer to consult them on health and safety issues which affect them.

This guide concentrates on good practice based on the above regulations and should apply to the majority of workplaces. However, the Offshore Installations (Safety Representatives and Safety Committees) Regulations 1989 apply to offshore workplaces.[3] There are also specific requirements to consult your employees or their health and safety representatives in other health and safety legislation which applies to specific industries.[1] Where it is more appropriate and relevant, you should refer to industry-specific guidance for your workplace.

Key to material

The guide is designed to clearly distinguish different types of information so you can find the parts which are relevant to you. For example:

■ references to the regulations are colour-coded (see the key below) and more information about who they apply to and the relationship between them is in paragraphs 14-18;
■ good practice advice and case studies feature throughout the guide and are highlighted;
■ checklists are used as reminders.

For workplaces where the Safety Representatives and Safety Committees Regulations 1977 apply.

For workplaces where the Health and Safety (Consultation with Employees) Regulations 1996 apply.

For workplaces where both the Safety Representatives and Safety Committees Regulations 1977 and the Health and Safety (Consultation with Employees) Regulations 1996 apply.

Overview

Consultation on health and safety is simply a two-way process between you and your employees where you:

- **talk** to each other about issues;
- **listen** to their concerns and raise your concerns;
- **seek** and **share** views and information;
- **discuss** issues in good time; and
- **consider** what employees say before you make decisions.

The guidance will take you through the process of how to consult your workforce, from getting started, to getting it right. We recognise you will be at different stages along the process, for example your starting point may be 'Get it right' rather than 'Get started'.

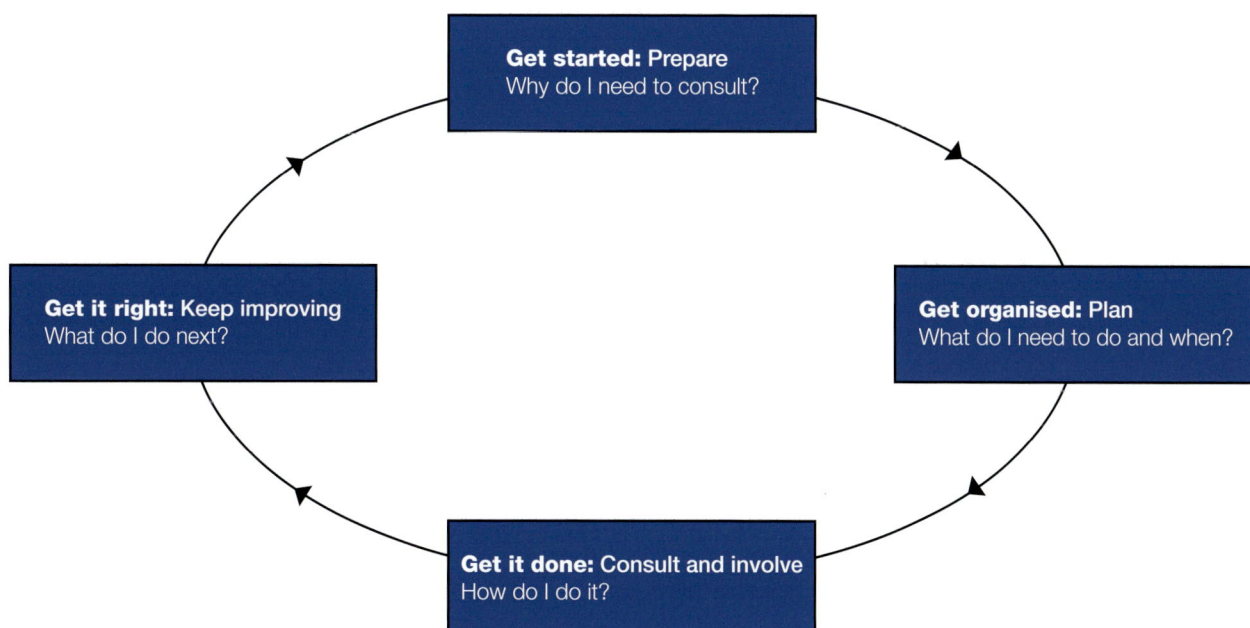

Get started: Prepare
Why do I need to consult?

Get organised: Plan
What do I need to do and when?

Get it done: Consult and involve
How do I do it?

Get it right: Keep improving
What do I do next?

Introduction

1   Health and safety at work is about securing the health, safety and welfare of people at work by reducing risks, and protecting them and others from harm or illness arising out of work activities by taking the right precautions. As an employer or manager, it is your duty to manage health and safety sensibly in your business, and involving your employees is at the very heart of this.

2   Current legislation[1] provides a framework of requirements for employee involvement in health and safety. You are required, under these regulations and other health and safety regulations, to give employees information, instruction and training, and engage in consultation with them about matters affecting their health and safety. Communication and consultation are the most basic forms of employee involvement in health and safety management. It is crucial that you get them right, not only because the law requires this but because they form the foundation for fully engaging your workforce to achieve the type of changes in behaviour in managers and employees that will lead to safer and healthier workplaces.

3   However, building on what is required by law enables you to create a genuine partnership between you and your employees and/or their representatives to manage health and safety risks. It creates a culture of collaboration where concerns, ideas and solutions are freely shared and acted upon, and where the whole workforce is engaged in promoting a healthy and safe environment. This means there is greater potential for improvements to health and safety for your business. In most cases effective consultation systems will generate levels of involvement that improve performance and raise standards.

4   Consultation and workforce involvement is not something you should be daunted by or discouraged about. It does not have to be lengthy and bureaucratic. If you have a small business, consultation can be an informal process of talking to your employees regularly and considering their views when you take decisions about health and safety. It can sometimes be more effective to have a simple process rather than something overly complicated. However, it is equally important that you do make time to talk and think together about issues more formally where this is necessary.

5   Consultation and involvement do not remove the right of employers and managers to manage. You must still make the final decision, but talking to your employees is an important part of successfully managing health and safety.

Get started: Prepare

6   This section is about preparing to involve your workforce. It explains:

- why you should talk to your employees about health and safety;
- what the law says and how it applies to your workplace; and
- how to gain commitment from the business and your workforce.

Why talk to your employees about health and safety?

The facts*

7   Accident rates are lower where employees genuinely feel they do have a say in health and safety matters than in workplaces where employees do not get involved.

8   Employee involvement in health and safety management relates to a more positive health and safety climate – 77% of employees felt encouraged to raise concerns in a good health and safety climate compared to 20% who felt encouraged to do so in a poor health and safety climate. In poor health and safety climates, accident rates are highest among workplaces where employees do not feel they can have a say.

9   Stronger employee involvement means better control of common workplace risks such as slips and trips – very effective in 76% of cases where employees felt they were always consulted but only very effective in 40% of cases if they thought they were rarely, or never, consulted.

10   Employers can learn about the risks through consultation – the risk of stress and slips and trips occur practically everywhere, but awareness of them is higher where there is employee involvement (62%) compared to where there is no involvement (28%).

11   Research has also shown that workplaces with health and safety committees where some members are selected by unions have significantly lower rates of work-related injury than those found in workplaces with no co-operative health and safety management.

12   Aside from your legal duty to consult, workplaces where employees are involved in taking decisions about health and safety are safer and healthier. Your employees influence health and safety through their own actions. They are often the best people to understand the risks in their workplace. Talking, listening and co-operating with each other can help:

- identify joint solutions to problems;
- develop a positive health and safety culture where risks are managed sensibly;
- reduce accidents and ill health, plus their related costs to your business;
- bring about improvements in overall efficiency, quality and productivity;
- meet customer demands and maintain credibility; and
- comply with legal requirements.

13   A workforce that feels valued and involved in decision-making plays a big part in a high-performing workplace. Empowering your workforce, giving them the right skills, and getting them involved in making decisions shows them that you take their health, safety and wellbeing seriously. They not only raise concerns but offer solutions too. There can be an impact far beyond health and safety management if the workforce is not engaged on health and safety issues which affect them.

What does the law say?

14   The law sets out how you must consult your employees in different situations and the different choices you have to make. There are two sets of general regulations about your duty to consult your workforce about health and safety:

- the Safety Representatives and Safety Committees Regulations 1977 (as amended);[1]
- the Health and Safety (Consultation with Employees) Regulations 1996 (as amended).[1]

---

* HSE *Fit3 (Fit for Work, Fit for Life, Fit for Tomorrow) employer and employee surveys 2005/06* (provisional results) and Nichols T, Walters D and Tasiran AC (2007) *Journal of Industrial Relations* **49**: 211-225.

Case study
Babcock Marine

Devonport Royal Dockyard committed to changing their health and safety culture using a number of initiatives to get the whole workforce involved in managing health and safety issues, ranging from working at height to radiation.

The challenge
In an industry with an established culture, the real challenge was making a commitment to develop a health and safety culture where the workforce is engaged and involved.

How has the health and safety culture been changed?
In 2006 a Safety Culture Team was formed and this includes an industrial health and safety representative on secondment from production. The trade union guidance group, involving proactive members from each union, look at groundroot safety, personal protective equipment (PPE), and better practice in risk assessments. They co-ordinate weekly safety meetings and also visit other companies to keep improving communication and joint working with the health and safety representatives.

Mike Tabb, Convenor and Health and Safety Representative, Amicus/Unite, said:

'This sounds long-winded but it works. Staff are starting to believe that management is serious about [health and] safety.'

How is the workforce involved in tackling health and safety?
- Staff take part in a 'Time Out for Safety' session every Monday at 11 am for thirty minutes. They are encouraged to bring any safety matters to the attention of the team leader and to discuss any ideas they have for safer working.
- The Accident Prevention Team of middle managers and health and safety representatives from each area meet once a month and deal with anything that cannot be dealt with at Time Out for Safety sessions.
- The Safety Improving Team, including the chair of the Accident Prevention Team and two senior health and safety representatives (both union and non-industrial representatives), then look at issues that the Accident Prevention Team cannot deal with – this group also meet on a monthly basis.
- The highest tier is at director level, the Executive Safety Improvement Group, who control the budget to make the changes in all health and safety matters. The meetings involve the top management and directors, but also involve the trade unions. They also liaise with the unions on policy changes.

Has the culture changed?
'It was a particular challenge to get workers to accept this culture change after 300 years of people believing they were working safely. And there are still the majority who believe the company is not seriously committed – but we are getting there!

'The big stick approach does not work. Only by working together can we succeed – we all have nothing to lose and everything to gain.'

Benefits so far
- Accidents have been reduced by 35%.
- Sickness absence is below 3%.

15 The flowchart (Figure 1) shows the relationship between the two sets of regulations and how they apply to you and your workforce. The regulations are designed to enable you and your employees to co-operate effectively in developing, maintaining and promoting measures that ensure health and safety at work, and to check the effectiveness of such measures. In some workplaces, for example where some employees are members of recognised trade unions and others are not, you may have to consult according to both sets of regulations. See paragraphs 34-36 for more information about this.

16 These regulations will apply to most workplaces, but do not apply to offshore installations, which are covered by separate guidance – see *A guide to the Offshore Installations (Safety Representatives and Safety Committees) Regulations 1989* (L110)[3] from HSE Books and the leaflet *Play your part!* (INDG421).[4] For examples of industry-specific regulations with requirements to consult your workforce, see *Consulting workers on health and safety*.[1]

17 The presence of a union health and safety representative does not prevent managers from communicating directly with the workforce as a whole. Managers remain responsible for managing health and safety in the workplace and should consult the workforce as necessary.

Figure 1 The law on consulting employees about health and safety in your workplace

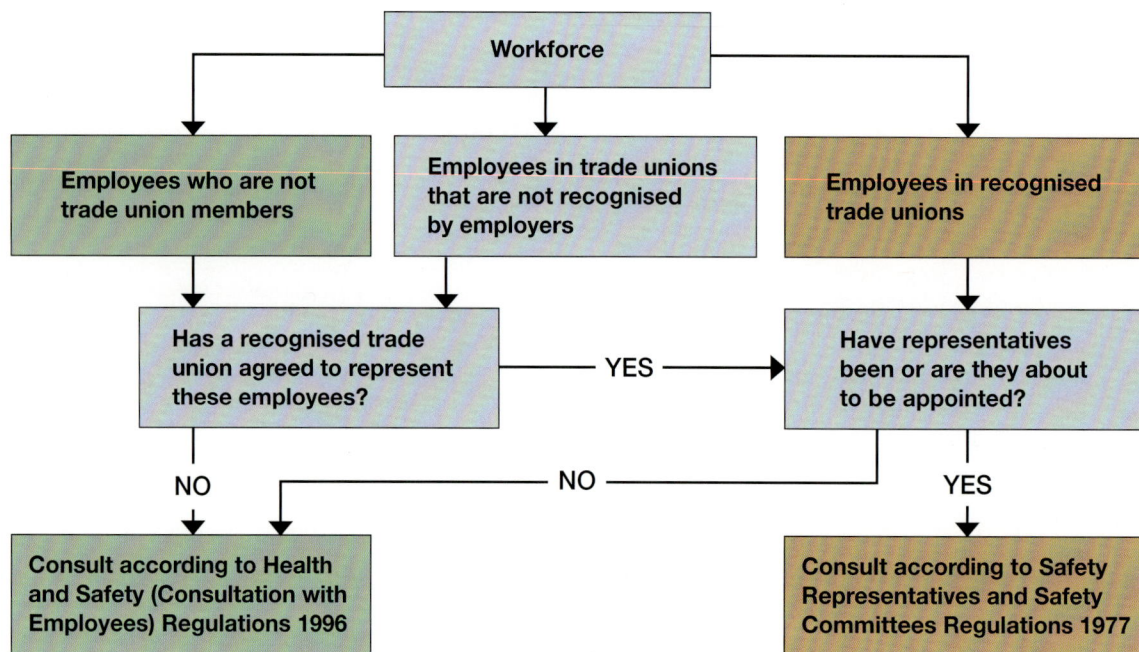

```
                              ┌──────────────────┐
                              │    Workforce     │
                              └──────────────────┘
        ┌───────────────────────────┼───────────────────────────┐
        ▼                           ▼                           ▼
┌─────────────────┐    ┌─────────────────────┐    ┌─────────────────┐
│ Employees who   │    │ Employees in trade  │    │ Employees in    │
│ are not trade   │    │ unions that are not │    │ recognised      │
│ union members   │    │ recognised by       │    │ trade unions    │
│                 │    │ employers           │    │                 │
└─────────────────┘    └─────────────────────┘    └─────────────────┘
        │                           │                           │
        ▼                           ▼                           ▼
        └───────┐    ┌──────────────────────┐      ┌─────────────────────┐
                ▼    ▼                        YES    ▼                     │
         ┌─────────────────────┐  ───────────────►  ┌─────────────────────┐
         │ Has a recognised    │                    │ Have representatives│
         │ trade union agreed  │                    │ been or are they    │
         │ to represent these  │                    │ about to be         │
         │ employees?          │                    │ appointed?          │
         └─────────────────────┘                    └─────────────────────┘
                │                                          │
               NO          ─────── NO ───────             YES
                ▼                                          ▼
   ┌───────────────────────────┐          ┌───────────────────────────┐
   │ Consult according to      │          │ Consult according to      │
   │ Health and Safety         │          │ Safety Representatives    │
   │ (Consultation with        │          │ and Safety Committees     │
   │ Employees) Regulations    │          │ Regulations 1977          │
   │ 1996                      │          │                           │
   └───────────────────────────┘          └───────────────────────────┘
```

In some workplaces you may have to consult under both sets of regulations (see paragraphs 34-36)

Key to colour-coded material

References to the regulations are colour-coded to help you find the parts that are most relevant to you:

For workplaces where the Safety Representatives and Safety Committees Regulations 1977 apply.

For workplaces where the Health and Safety (Consultation with Employees) Regulations 1996 apply.

For workplaces where both the Safety Representatives and Safety Committees Regulations 1977 and the Health and Safety (Consultation with Employees) Regulations 1996 apply.

18 Where you already have existing consultation arrangements that satisfy health and safety law, there is no requirement to change them. However, you may want to review your arrangements to make sure that they are the right ones for your organisation now.

19 If there are any disagreements between you and your employees about the interpretation of these regulations, they should, to begin with, be addressed through the normal machinery for resolving employment relations disputes. In certain circumstances, it may be helpful to involve the Arbitration and Conciliation Service (Acas); see the 'Sources of advice' section at the back of the book for contact details. However, health and safety inspectors (from HSE and local authorities) can enforce for failure to comply with legal duties on procedural matters. They will decide what action to take in line with HSE's *Enforcement policy statement* (see www.hse.gov.uk/enforce).[5]

Consulting where the Safety Representatives and Safety Committees Regulations 1977 apply

20 If you recognise trade unions in any part of the business then:

- the Safety Representatives and Safety Committees Regulations 1977 will apply;
- the trade union may **appoint** health and safety representatives (referred to as 'safety representatives' in the regulations); and
- you **must** consult the union-appointed health and safety representatives on health and safety matters affecting the employees they represent. For more information on what you must consult them about, see paragraph 53.

21 You may have:

- different representatives from the same union for different parts of the business;
- different representatives from different unions for different parts of the business;
- union representatives representing employees who belong to other unions by agreement with the other unions; and
- union representatives representing employees who are not union members.

22 Recognised unions and employers should discuss the number of health and safety representatives the union will appoint. This will depend on different factors, eg the size of your business. If there are differences of opinion that need to be resolved, use your existing employment relations processes or contact Acas for help. For more information about the functions of union-appointed health and safety representatives see www.hse.gov.uk/involvement.

23 The nature of your business could mean that you and trade unions will have to be more flexible about the group or groups of employees represented and the number of representatives suitable for your workplace. For example:

- when there are rapidly changing situations and conditions in a workplace as work develops, or frequent changes in the numbers of employees (eg on

building and construction sites, in shipbuilding and ship repairing, docks, and factories);
- if most of your employees go out to their actual place of work somewhere else but report back to you (eg goods and freight depots, builders' yards, and service depots of all kinds);
- if a workplace in one location has a wide variety of work activities going on (eg retail stores, hospitals, and manufacturing plants);
- where workplaces have particularly high process risks (eg construction sites at particular stages like demolition or excavations, and some chemical works and research establishments);
- if the majority of employees are employed in low-risk activities, but one or two processes or activities or items of plant have special risks connected with them;
- where there is a mix of direct employees and others in the workplace such as contract and agency workers;
- where there is a mix of employees who are members of trade unions and those who are not.

24 Normally, trade unions will write to inform you of who the appointed health and safety representative is, and make it clear which groups of employees the representative is representing. An appointed representative should usually have worked for you for the previous two years, or had at least two years' experience doing similar work. This is to ensure they will have a level of knowledge that allows them to make a responsible and practical contribution to the health and safety effort. However, there may also be times when it is not practical to appoint a representative with two years' experience in your organisation or in the job, for instance if:

- you are a new employer or the location is newly established;
- the work is of a short duration; or
- there is a high turnover of employees.

25 In such cases, trade unions will appoint the most appropriate representatives, taking their experience and skills into account.

26 If two or more union health and safety representatives ask in writing for a health and safety committee, you must set one up within three months. See paragraphs 125-146 for more information on health and safety committees.

Consulting where the Health and Safety (Consultation with Employees) Regulations 1996 apply

27 The law is different if there are employees who are not represented under the Safety Representatives and Safety Committee Regulations 1977, for example if:

- you do not recognise trade unions;
- you do recognise trade unions but representatives have not been appointed or are not about to be appointed; or
- there are any employees who do not belong to a trade union and recognised trade unions have not agreed to represent them.

28 Where employees are not represented under the Safety Representatives and Safety Committees Regulations 1977, the Health and Safety (Consultation with Employees) Regulations 1996 will apply.

Individuals and representatives

29 You can choose to consult employees directly as individuals, or through **elected** health and safety representatives (known as 'representatives of employee safety' in the Regulations), or a combination of the two.

30 If you have a small business, or you have regular contact with all your employees, then consulting with individuals is often effective. It gives everyone a chance to have a say in health and safety matters. However, consulting individuals is not practical for all businesses, and consultation through elected representatives may work better.

Electing representatives

31 The size or spread of your workforce may make it unrealistic to consult everyone individually. You may want to arrange for your employees to elect representatives of their choice. See www.hse.gov.uk/involvement for more information on elections and the functions of health and safety representatives elected by the workforce.

32 Although by law health and safety representatives appointed by trade unions have more functions than representatives elected by employees, you can choose to give your elected representatives extra roles as well, as long as they agree to this (see paragraph 35).

33 If you are consulting more than a few representatives, then it is better to do so in a structured forum like a health and safety committee, joint consultative committee, or works council. See paragraphs 125-146 for more information.

Consulting where both the Safety Representatives and Safety Committees Regulations 1977 and the Health and Safety (Consultation with Employees) Regulations 1996 apply

34 A range of workforce structures and arrangements exist in workplaces so it is not unusual to have some parts of a business where employees are members of recognised trade unions and others where they are not. In this case, you may have to consult both:

- health and safety representatives appointed by recognised trade unions under the Safety Representatives and Safety Committees Regulations 1977 (see paragraph 20); and
- the remainder of your workforce, either directly where practical, or through elected health and safety representatives under the Health and Safety (Consultation with Employees) Regulations 1996 (see paragraphs 27-28).

35 Where you have both union-appointed representatives and employee-elected health and safety representatives, it is good practice to:

- consult both together about health and safety matters which affect the employees they represent through a joint health and safety committee where both types of representatives are members. See paragraph 131 and the UCATT case study after paragraph 146 for more information;
- involve and consult health and safety representatives elected by the workforce in joint inspections and investigations as you would the union-appointed health and safety representatives. See paragraphs 108-113 and the Springfield Fuels case study after paragraph 127 for more information.

36 It is simpler and better to consult health and safety representatives at the same time about the same issues where possible. Joint involvement leads to joint problem solving.

Good practice

37 Where a trade union is not recognised or has not appointed a health and safety representative, or there are employees who are not represented by a union, ask your workforce if they would like to be consulted directly, through representatives, or a combination of the two, and how regularly consultation should take place. If it is not practical to consult directly or employees would like representatives, you should arrange for them to be elected.

Employment protection

38 All your employees are protected by employment law against suffering any harm because of any reasonable actions they take on health and safety grounds (under the Employment Rights Act 1996, as amended). This applies regardless of their length of service. Employees, including health and safety representatives, should not suffer harm, for instance by being denied a promotion or being dismissed unfairly, because they:

- carry out, or propose to carry out, activities that you have assigned to them in connection with preventing or reducing health and safety risks;
- perform, or propose to perform, functions they have as union-appointed or employee-elected health and safety representatives, or health and safety committee members;
- stand as a candidate in an election to be an employee representative or participate in the election by voting;
- bring to your attention, by reasonable means, a concern about circumstances at work which they reasonably believe are harmful, or potentially harmful, to health and safety;
- reasonably believe a situation to be of serious and imminent danger and, because they could not reasonably be expected to avert it, they leave or propose to leave the workplace or any dangerous part of it, or if they refuse to return while the danger continues; and
- reasonably believe a situation to be of serious and imminent danger, and take or propose to take

appropriate steps to protect themselves and others. This is to be judged by looking at all the circumstances, including knowledge, facilities and advice, available at the time.

39 Employers could be taken to an employment tribunal if they penalise employees in this way. Further information about employment rights and unfair dismissal can be found at www.berr.gov.uk.

How do you gain commitment to involving your workforce?

40 Commitment from all sides is vital for employee involvement to be effective and successful in making improvements to health and safety. This means you, your employees, and trade unions where they are recognised, need to gain buy-in to the process.

Get commitment from the business

41 If you are in charge of a business or responsible for managing health and safety, you might need to convince others in management to commit. Leadership and commitment from management is important in making involvement successful. Apart from the legal duty to consult, you can demonstrate why this is something you should be doing by building a case in a number of ways:

- highlight how co-operating with employees in other areas of the business has led to improvements;
- demonstrate evidence of the benefits to the business (see some of the case studies in this guide or on HSE's worker involvement web pages (www.hse.gov.uk/involvement);
- look at current health and safety issues which could be addressed through consultation. For example, if you see an increase in a particular type of injury, discuss the best way to address it with staff;
- explain that engaging the workforce is an investment, and it may take time to develop trust, but it has been shown to reduce workplace injuries and accidents; and
- provide reassurance that it will not diminish effective management because consultation does not mean you have to agree about every issue, but rather discuss the areas of disagreement and respect the views of others.

Get commitment from your employees

42 Employees are more likely to engage and believe in consultation when senior managers show personal and long-term commitment, and listen to the views of employees because they want to hear what the workforce has to say. Real belief in the benefits of involving your workforce creates co-operation as well as complying with your legal duty.

43 Your employees are more likely to communicate with you if:

- they are committed to your business goals, including the health and safety goals;
- they think it is in their interests to participate;
- they trust you and find you approachable; and
- your actions match your words.

Encouraging employees to be a health and safety representative

44 The workforce may have reservations about performing the role of a health and safety representative, particularly in non-unionised workplaces. Employees may believe that:

- health and safety is a matter for individuals;
- they will be punished for criticising management practice;
- they lack the skills and confidence to take on the role; or
- you will not truly take on board their concerns.

45 To encourage employees to represent colleagues on health and safety issues, you can build commitment in your workforce by:

- clearly stating your intention to discuss matters affecting employee health and safety with them as required in your health and safety policy statement;
- explaining the benefits of joint working and co-operation for everyone because everyone has a role to play in addressing health and safety;
- ensuring there is a safe environment to raise issues by respecting the views of the workforce;
- showing how you will consider what they have to say by providing feedback to explain how decisions take employee views into account; and

- allowing them to have a say and make a difference in the decision-making process.

46 On an **individual** level, provide:

- appropriate training to develop skills and confidence (see paragraphs 75-78);
- access to suitable support networks, for example through RoSPA's regional Safety Groups UK networks (see www.safetygroupsuk.org.uk for more information);
- opportunities to demonstrate how valuable their contribution is through recognition, for example in performance agreements or rewards such as a corporate award for health and safety representative of the year.

47 As you demonstrate your commitment to workforce involvement in health and safety, it will develop your workforce's commitment. This helps to build the trust, co-operation and communication you need to make it work.

Good practice

48 Train your managers, supervisors and health and safety representatives together and clearly identify their roles in health and safety, enabling them all to see things from a shared perspective.

Case study

Overcoming challenges to worker involvement

A truck manufacturer in the north-east wanted to capitalise on the knowledge of their workers in managing noise and vibration issues but knew they would have to rise to the challenge if they were to reap the benefits.

The challenge
A project to tackle hand-arm vibration issues was only going to work if management could gain workers' trust and co-operation. They realised this was not going to be easily achieved when workers were asked to keep a record of what tools they used and for how long – only four forms from a workforce of 78 were returned.

Overcoming the problem
From the poor response rate, management quickly realised that their staff were suspicious about why they were being asked to record the information requested. They learned that workers' trust was vital before they could really get them involved in what they were trying to do.

So they arranged for some training to raise awareness of the health issues involved when using vibrating hand tools and explained that they couldn't fully address the situation without their workers' help.

The Project Leader said:

'We assured them that what we were doing certainly wasn't a front for some kind of time and motion survey! The result – nearly everyone filled in and returned their forms.'

By talking to the workers and involving them in solving the problem, the company found out that workers become 'attached' to their hand tools. If they did the job well, they'd continue to use them, no matter how old the tools were or how much vibration they caused.

Towards joint problem solving
A tool amnesty was held, production lines were re-tooled with efficient, low-vibration equipment and workers were told about the risk and how to avoid it.

'When you start to involve workers, you learn such a lot about the problems and issues they face during their working day. The whole point of worker involvement is that you need to listen to what your people have got to say and get them involved in developing the solutions.'

Suggestion scheme
The company set up a suggestion scheme, complete with boards around the production line where staff can raise any issue they like. Every week, teams check the boards, note any suggestions that come under their area of responsibility, and consider what action they can take. A staff member's suggestion card remains on the board until they are happy it's been acted on – only they can remove it.

And the result?
They've had hundreds of suggestions in the six months the boards have been up, and made dozens of improvements as a result.

'The changes we've seen over the last 12 months have been incredible. At first, workers weren't sure exactly what this initiative was about, but once we saw improvements being made, everyone soon got on board.

'As a result, we now have fewer absences, a happier workforce, and quality and productivity are up. Every company should get its workers involved.'

Get organised: Plan

49 This section will help you to plan effectively and covers:

- what affects how you involve your workforce;
- what you should consult your workforce about;
- when you should consult so that you do it in good time; and
- arrangements for training health and safety representatives.

What affects how you involve your workforce?

50 When planning how best to involve your employees, you need to consider the following factors about the business, the workplace and the workforce that will have an impact on how you can engage your employees.

The business
- Structure of the business.
- Management style.
- Organisational and safety cultures.
- Trade union recognition and employment relations.

The workplace
- Size of workplace.
- Location of sites.
- Types of work done.
- Degree and nature of inherent dangers.

The workforce
- Size of workforce.
- Diversity of the workforce.
- Employment structures (eg direct employees, agency and contract workers).
- Work patterns such as shift systems, part-time etc.
- Offsite, remote or mobile workers.

51 These factors will affect whether you consult individuals or representatives, the methods you use, organisation of inspections and investigations, and co-ordination between committees, among other things. For example, a high-risk, unionised workplace with a large workforce spread over multiple sites may have union representatives from each site as a member of a site-based health and safety committee that meets regularly, and feeds into a corporate health and safety committee. A non-unionised, smaller workplace, located on one small, low-risk site, is more likely to consult directly with employees on a day-to-day basis.

What should you be consulting your workforce about?

52 The law says that you must consult your workforce about anything in the workplace that could substantially affect their health and safety. The specifics will vary from workplace to workplace.

53 In general, you **must** consult about:

- any change which may have a substantial affect on your workforce's health and safety. Such changes may include new or different procedures, types of work, equipment, premises, and ways of working (eg new shift patterns);
- your arrangements for getting competent people to help you meet your obligations under health and safety laws, for example the appointment of a health and safety manager. For more information about what a competent person is, see paragraphs 59-60;
- information you must give your workforce on the likely risks in their work and precautions they should take. Discuss with employees and representatives the best way for information to be shared. Consider issues of language, literacy and learning disabilities if appropriate (see paragraphs 103-105 for more information);
- the planning of health and safety training; and
- the health and safety consequences of introducing new technology.

Risk assessments

54 You have a legal duty to assess the risks to the health and safety of your employees (and risks to the health and safety of people not in your employment) which they are exposed to while they are at work.

55 In carrying out a risk assessment, you should consult employees and health and safety representatives. It is a valuable way of involving the staff that do the work. They know the risks involved and scope for potentially dangerous short cuts and problems. Employees are more likely to understand why procedures are put in place to control risks and follow them if they have been involved in the process of developing health and safety practices in their workplace.

56 This does not mean that formal consultation is required before every task-specific assessment conducted in workplaces. It simply means that consultation should form part of the general risk assessment process. In practice, most employers conduct a general assessment to identify the key risks and control measures, and then a second brief assessment of the risks by the employees about to embark on the job.

57 Consulting employees and representatives on risk assessments is covered in L21 *Management of health and safety at work*.[6]

58 For further information about the requirements to consult health and safety representatives and employees about information, instruction and training, as well as the requirements in existing health and safety legislation, see L146 *Consulting workers on health and safety*.[1]

59 You must get help from a competent person to enable you to meet the requirements of health and safety law. A competent person is someone who has sufficient training and experience or knowledge and other qualities that allow them to assist you properly. The level of competence required will depend on the complexity of the situation and the particular help you need.

60 When getting help, you should give preference to those in your own organisation who have the appropriate level of competence (which can include employers themselves) before looking for help from outside. You are required to consult health and safety representatives in good time on the arrangements for competent help. For more information, see L21 *Management of health and safety at work*.[6]

Good practice

61 Don't limit the scope of consultation to a pre-set list because there will be times when you should involve employees about issues which are not on the list.

62 Consult and involve employees and health and safety representatives on:

- accident and investigations reports, risk assessments, and emergency plans;
- occupational health issues including what the provision (for employees) is and how effective it is; and
- the nature of the post, knowledge and experience suitable for the role of your competent person (eg health and safety manager).

63 It is good practice to provide feedback to explain decisions and respond to issues raised by employees or their representatives. The appropriate method of responding (in writing or verbally), and reasonable timescales for providing a response, will depend on the nature and circumstances of the issue and the workplace. The arrangements should be agreed with your employees or their representatives in advance.

64 Employee involvement is a good way to address work-related health issues, particularly if you have usually involved people more on safety matters in the past. Health issues, like stress in the workplace or musculoskeletal disorders, are areas where your employees can add value in helping you to address them.

Case study

BT Group plc

BT has over 100 000 employees working in six different lines of business, spanning 170 countries. Full engagement is always a challenge, but BT sought to address health and wellbeing issues affecting their workforce by getting them involved.

The challenge

In common with many other organisations, mental health is one of the growing risks at BT. Stress is a significant cause of time away from work and BT see addressing health and wellbeing issues as important for their people, the business and society. The aim was to enhance employee involvement in managing health issues to improve the health of employees and facilitate joint problem solving. It also helps to drive down costs associated with mental-health-related absenteeism, and reduced productivity, and furthers BT's corporate social responsibility credentials.

Working with health and safety representatives

The Communication Workers Union (CWU) and Connect have an agreement with BT which covers the role of health and safety representatives, formalises arrangements for training, and fosters co-operation between management and employee representatives. Their partnership with management enables health and safety issues to be addressed in a non-political and non-confrontational manner. For example, BT's health and safety representatives worked with managers to form and promote a strategy on tackling health issues.

Getting the workforce on board

BT has wellbeing leads in each line of the business. They, along with specialists in health and safety and communications, tailor the messages about the importance of health issues and cascade them to the workforce to raise awareness. For instance, the Retail business use their radio channel and the plasma screens in their contact centres, and the Openreach business use their in-house magazine. Three months after one education initiative, the

Positive Mentality campaign, the follow-up online survey results showed that, of those who had accessed the materials:

- 68% learned something new about ways to look after their mental health;
- 56% tried some of the recommendations and continued to practise them at the time of the survey;
- 51% of those who had made changes had noticed improvements in their mental health and wellbeing.

BT's strategy for mental wellbeing

The strategy consists of three phases:

- proactively promoting good mental health and reducing risks to mental wellbeing at source through workplace and job design;
- identifying early signs of mental ill health and supporting individuals to address any work or non-work pressures;
- helping people suffering from mental ill health to cope and recover.

The strategy has resulted in initiatives that promote good health, prevent ill health, identify those at risk and provide early intervention.

Benefits so far

Quantifiable benefits are often difficult to demonstrate in the short term as impact really depends on a comprehensive, integrated longer-term approach. However, over the past four to five years, the sickness absence rate due to mental health problems has fallen by 30% despite pressured market conditions.

BT now gets almost 80% of people who have been off for more than six months with mental illness back into their own jobs, compared with 20% nationally.

Dr Catherine Kilfedder, BT's Group Health Adviser, says:

'On the health and wellbeing side, all the evidence suggests that a participative approach, a not 'done to' but 'done with' approach, is most effective.

'All of our health promotion initiatives are developed in conjunction with the CWU and Connect, in partnership with a relevant non-governmental organisation (NGO), then cascaded through our lines of business by the wellbeing and communications leads. Where possible, we try to identify a senior business champion who will provide high-level visibility and promotion for these initiatives.

'We think it is important to identify and utilise your 'champions', those with interest and enthusiasm for the area.'

When should you consult?

Good practice

65   Commit to involving employees and health and safety representatives promptly and as a matter of routine. It develops a shared understanding of the key issues and how to address them.

66   There is no legal set time limit but you must consult **in good time**. This means there has to be enough time to explain the issues to employees, time for them to consider and get back to you with informed responses, and time for you to take into account their response before you make a final decision.

67   It is advisable to consult promptly and regularly. Regular consultation is better than consulting on a case-by-case basis as issues come up because it allows you to spot potential problems early.

68   How long the consultation process takes will largely depend on the complexity of what you are asking the workforce to consider, how many people you are consulting, and methods of consultation. A simple issue where you need to consult a smaller number of representatives can probably be dealt with in a few days or addressed routinely through regular channels of consultation. A technical matter requiring time for consideration, or consulting an entire large workforce, is likely to require longer.

Good practice

69   Agree to respond to the issues raised by your employees and their representatives within a certain time frame and share the reasons for your decisions with them. It will demonstrate that you are committed and how you have considered what they say.

70   For unexpected issues you will not have had time to plan consultation so consider if the issue can be addressed through one of your normal consultation methods, or if you need to do something different like hold a one-off meeting. The key is to work these matters into your consultation process so that you do listen to the views of your workforce and the issue is not overlooked.

71   Have procedures in place for settling disagreements about health and safety with employees or their representatives. Consultation will not always result in agreement but you should be able to resolve differences of opinion by being open, explaining the reasons behind decisions, and following agreed procedures for resolving problems.

Training arrangements for health and safety representatives

72   For health and safety representatives to be able to perform their role, they need to be equipped with appropriate skills and knowledge, so you must plan for their training.

Training for health and safety representatives appointed by trade unions

73 If you have health and safety representatives appointed by trade unions, the trade union will make the necessary arrangements.

74 Trade unions do offer online training courses so health and safety representatives may not always have to leave the workplace, but may simply require access to online training and time to complete the course.

Training for elected health and safety representatives

75 If your workforce has elected health and safety representatives, you must ensure they are provided with time off with pay to undergo training that is reasonable in all the circumstances (see paragraph 88).

Identify training needs
76 It will be helpful for all new health and safety representatives to have training that will cover:

- the role of the representative, including how to communicate in committee meetings, with colleagues for views, with employers to raise issues, and with health and safety inspectors;
- health and safety legislation;
- how to identify and minimise hazards and dangerous occurrences;
- health and safety issues of new technology; and
- how to carry out a workplace inspection and accident investigation (not required but recommended for employee elected representatives).

Suppliers

77 You can approach a number of bodies for advice to explore suitable training options. These include:

- The National Examination Board in Occupational Safety and Health (Nebosh);
- Institution of Occupational Safety and Health (IOSH);
- The Royal Society for the Prevention of Accidents (RoSPA);
- The British Safety Council;
- ENTO – Network of National Training Organisations;
- trade union colleges;
- trade associations;
- local adult learning colleges;
- your local authority, who may run health and safety training courses; and
- the Health and Safety Laboratory (HSL).

78 The above list is not exhaustive, and there are other training providers that you can find locally through your own research or recommendations from others.

Checklist for planning workforce involvement and consultation

✓ Confirm which set of regulations applies to your workplace – in some cases both could apply.

✓ Ensure you and your representatives have the time, resources, and facilities to adequately consult and involve your employees.

✓ If you recognise a trade union, identify who the union-appointed health and safety representatives are and let your employees know.

✓ If you have employees not being represented by union-appointed representatives:
   ✓ decide whether you will consult your workforce directly as individuals if practical, or through elected representatives;
   ✓ arrange to hold elections if consulting through representatives (see www.hse.gov.uk/involvement); and
   ✓ make arrangements for training your representatives.

✓ Be clear on what you have to consult your workforce about.

✓ Arrange to consult your workforce in good time so that you can consider their input before you make a decision.

✓ Consider the most appropriate methods to consult your workforce – this could be a joint forum involving union-appointed health and safety representatives and employee-elected representatives if both sets of regulations apply in your workplace.

✓ Agree a process of responding to your employees or their representatives.

✓ Prepare material for consultations, for example meeting agendas or intranet pages.

✓ Arrange processes to handle any potential disagreements between you and employees or their representatives.

✓ If you have both union-appointed representatives and representatives elected by your workforce, follow all the above.

Get it done: Consult and involve

79   This section provides practical advice on ways to consult and involve your employees or their representatives. It explains:

- what your duties are when consulting representatives;
- methods of involving your employees;
- how to involve representatives in investigations and inspections; and
- how to set up a health and safety committee and make it work well.

What are your duties when consulting health and safety representatives?

80   You have a duty to:

- allow representatives paid time to perform their role and to undertake training;
- provide facilities and assistance;
- provide information; and
- if you recognise trade unions, set up a health and safety committee if two union-appointed representatives request it in writing.

Allow representatives paid time to perform their role

81   If you have union-appointed health and safety representatives or representatives elected by employees in your workplace, then you have a duty to:

- let them have time with pay as is necessary to carry out their role during their normal working hours; and
- let them have time with pay as is necessary to be trained to perform aspects of their role, as is reasonable in the circumstances.

Good practice

82   Performing the role of a health and safety representative is a part of their job once they have been appointed or elected. You can recognise this by recording it in the representatives' job description, work objectives or performance agreement for the year. In this way, you are allowing them to build in time to perform their role as part of their paid work, and making sure you are aware of the contribution they are making to the workplace.

83   Involve your elected health and safety representatives in inspections, investigations, risk assessments, and health and safety committee meetings.

84   Training for health and safety representatives is vital to enable them to carry out their roles effectively. You should follow the provisions in the regulations, so for more information see L146 *Consulting workers on health and safety*.[1] This is very important, because failure to allow paid time as is necessary to attend training or perform their roles could result in an employment tribunal.

85 If you have a union-appointed health and safety representative, the union will arrange and pay for their training and relevant travel and subsistence costs in most cases. In some situations, they may ask for employers to pay some costs, for example if the union is providing joint training on behalf of the employer.

86 Unions will decide what training their appointed health and safety representative will need, but there does need to be agreement between you and the unions on how the training is arranged to ensure smooth running of your business.

87 You should take account of the Approved Code of Practice and case law in this area.[1]

88 If you have elected representatives, then you have to pay the reasonable cost of their training, including travel and subsistence. During the election process you also have to allow candidates reasonable time with pay to carry out their functions as a candidate.

Provide facilities and assistance

89 You must provide your representatives with facilities they may reasonably need to carry out their role. Although the needs of health and safety representatives will vary from workplace to workplace, in general you should make sure they have **access to** equipment and assistance such as:

- a telephone and office area where they can have a private and confidential conversation as part of their role;
- suitable storage space for paperwork, records or reference material, such as a lockable cabinet or desk;
- intranet and internet facilities;
- communication and distribution facilities like a photocopier and a notice board to circulate information to the employees they represent; and
- time with you or senior management to discuss health and safety issues whenever the representative might reasonably need to.

90 You should also allow representatives to have facilities for investigation of hazards, complaints, and incidents, including private discussions with employees. This does not mean that you or your management representative cannot be on the premises at the time of the investigation.

Provide information

91 You have to provide any health and safety information that you have which will let your health and safety representatives fulfil their role. You should already have relevant health and safety information as part of your health and safety management system, such as copies of risk assessments or accident records. You **do not** need to present this information in a different format and provide it as a separate package, or get hold of additional information specifically for your employee representatives.

92 Health and safety representatives appointed by trade unions may ask to inspect and take copies of any document relating to workplace health and safety, or to employees they represent, although this does not apply to a health record of an identifiable individual unless the individual has given consent.

93 You should give your employees and representatives information that lets them understand:

- what the risks and dangers are for their work, or could be if there are changes to their work which will affect health and safety;
- what is done, or will be done, to reduce or stop the risks and dangers;
- what they ought to do when they come across a risk or dangerous situation; and
- the name of the competent person.

94 By law, you do **not** have to give employees or their representatives any information that:

- would be against the interests of national security or against the law;
- is about someone who has not given their permission for it to be shared;
- would harm the business unless it has an effect on health, safety or welfare; or
- is connected with legal proceedings.

Set up a health and safety committee

95 If two or more union-appointed safety representatives request in writing that you set up a health and safety committee, then you must do so within three months of the request being made. For advice on how to set up a committee and guidance on making it work, see the health and safety committees section at paragraphs 125-146.

Good practice

96 If you have two or more elected representatives, you can consult them through a health and safety committee too, although the law does not require you to do this. If you consult both union-appointed representatives and employee-elected representatives, have both of them represented on a health and safety committee.

What are the best ways to involve your employees?

97 The method you use to involve your employees will depend on:

- which regulations apply to your workplace;
- whether you are involving individuals directly or consulting your employee representatives; and
- the specific health and safety issue you wish to consult on.

98 The different methods of consulting your employees include:

- face to face, directly with individuals;
- indirectly with employees; and
- with representatives.

99 Use a range of methods to suit the circumstances and use a combination if a single method is not suitable. Whatever method you choose, you need to ensure it complies with your duties. For example, if you choose to consult with employees directly, you need to make sure it is practical, otherwise you must consult with representatives. There are various ways you can consult with employees face to face:

- **One-to-one discussions** can be particularly effective if you have a small business and have the opportunity to talk to your employees regularly.
- If your business is larger, then you could try **regular walkabouts** where you get to meet employees face to face, and they get to share ideas and concerns. If you are regularly approachable, employees are more likely to open up about the risks, especially if you then do something about the issues raised.
- Have **health and safety as a standing item** on the agenda of routine team meetings where your employees' views can be fed back to you, and so there is always an opportunity for health and safety issues to be picked up.
- **Special workforce meetings** can be best when you need to call the whole workforce together for their views and opinions. This could be in addition to regular team meetings. At large meetings, the exchange of views and ideas might not be as effective as in smaller gatherings where people may feel more comfortable sharing their views.

- **Arrange toolbox talks** where you have short talks on specific health and safety issues that show the relevance of a topic to particular jobs, for instance a talk about manual handling for those doing jobs that involve lifting heavy goods. It allows you and your workers to explore the risks and think about ways to deal with them.
- **Set up work groups** to tackle specific health and safety issues and explore ways of making a difference. The employees involved in the group should be directly involved with the issues being looked at so they can really contribute to solutions.

100 There are also indirect ways you can involve employees:

- **Company intranet sites** with health and safety information are convenient as they can feature news and request the views of all your staff. Keep the information updated and draw attention to new material so people who do not regularly check it will know what is happening in their workplace. If some staff do not have access to the site, the quality and range of views given may be compromised.
- **Staff surveys** can be useful in consulting your workforce, although a lack of trust can undermine surveys and reduce the return rate. Consider the literacy or language skills of the workers to make sure they can answer questions they understand. You can get an external organisation to run the staff survey so your employees feel they can say what they really think.
- **Employee suggestion schemes** can be useful if they are regularly used and acted upon (see the case study on overcoming challenges after paragraph 48). However, they may not work if employees believe they will not make a difference, or because you and your employees have already developed a good working relationship without the need for a suggestion box.
- **Notice boards and newsletters** can be useful for sharing information as part of the consultation process, particularly if used together with other methods as this increases the chance of getting your messages across.

101 Think about the different work patterns of the modern workplace. You may employ homeworkers, part-time workers, shiftworkers, and use agency workers and others, so think about the best way to consult them all.

102 Ask your employees or their representatives about their needs and preferences. Consulting them in a way that suits them as well as you shows that you want to hear what they have to say and will help them engage in the process.

Consulting and involving employees whose first language is not English

103 If your employees have difficulties understanding English, or employees have low literacy levels, there are a number of ways you can communicate with them to encourage their involvement. The aim is to achieve the same standard of understanding and involvement as for an English speaker. The following can help to involve and consult such employees:

■ ensure adequate time to consult with employees where language and/or literacy may be issues so they can absorb the information and respond to you;
■ encourage employees to express their views in their preferred language by using interpreters;
■ ask a work colleague to interpret, although these employees may need training if they are asked to undertake this role;
■ get information translated and check that this has been done clearly;
■ use pictorial information and internationally understood pictorial signs where appropriate;
■ where information has to be in English, use clear and simple materials, and allow more time;
■ committees and representatives should reflect the workforce they represent;
■ consider ESOL (English for Speakers of Other Languages) courses, as an improved grasp of English will help communication in the workplace and on health and safety.

104 Be aware of cultural differences and take these into account when consulting employees because there may be some employees who do not feel able to speak up about health and safety matters.

105 The key to individual consultation is to make sure that everybody is involved so you will have to choose methods carefully to encourage all members of the workforce.

Ways you can consult with representatives

106 You can still use some of the same methods to consult representatives that you would use to consult individuals if they are suitable, for example one-to-one meetings with the relevant representative. However, consultation with representatives is best carried out through a proper forum. You can do this in a number of ways:

■ Have a dedicated health and safety committee. They are particularly effective if you have several representatives for different groups, larger numbers of employees, both union-appointed representatives and employee-elected representatives, or representatives responsible for more than one site. For more information see paragraphs 125-146.
■ You may already be consulting your employees about other issues affecting the business and workforce through systems, for example through a joint consultative committee or works council. You may decide these are suitable ways to consult your employee representatives about health and safety too. However, you must make sure that you consider health and safety matters properly and they are not just added to a lengthy agenda that cannot do them justice. For more information about joint consultative committees and works councils visit the Acas website (www.acas.org.uk) or see their advisory booklet *Employee communications and consultation*.[7]

Investigation and inspection

107 Health and safety representatives appointed by trade unions have prescribed functions that you must involve them in, including:

■ investigating accidents, potential hazards and complaints; and
■ inspections of the workplace.

108 It is good practice to involve representatives that your employees have elected in joint investigations and inspections too.

Investigating accidents, hazards and complaints

109 Agree a system for informing the representative if an incident occurs and involve them in investigations as soon as possible. Such incidents can be vital signals that your way of preventing or reducing risks and dangers is not working. Proper investigation can show you where the weaknesses are so you can work towards improving the measures you take.

Good practice

110 An investigation involving the health and safety representative can give employees more confidence to co-operate. They may feel more comfortable speaking to a co-worker who can relate to them so they will say what they really think. Representatives can play a very useful role here in communicating effectively with you and your employees.

Inspections of the workplace

111 Formal inspections can take different forms and you and your representatives will need to agree the best methods for your workplace. Some of the ways inspections can take place, either separately or in combination over a period of time, are:

- safety tours – general inspections of the workplace;
- safety sampling – systematic sampling of particular dangerous activities, processes or areas;
- safety surveys – general inspections of particular dangerous activities, processes or areas; and
- incident inspections – carried out after an accident causing a fatality, injury or near miss which could have resulted in an injury or case of ill health and has been reported to the health and safety enforcing authority.

112 Sample forms you and your safety representatives may find helpful are available on the HSE website for:

- recording that an inspection by a safety representative has taken place (Form F2534);[8] and
- notifying you that there are unsafe or unhealthy conditions or working practices, and unsatisfactory arrangements for welfare at work (Form F2533).[9]

113 Where a health and safety representative has drawn your attention to the findings of an inspection they have carried out, you should consider the matter and decide what appropriate follow-up action should be taken.

Inspecting the workplace

114 Health and safety representatives appointed by trade unions can inspect the workplace. They have to give reasonable notice in writing when they intend to carry out a formal inspection, and have not inspected it in the previous three months.

115 If there is substantial change in conditions of work or new information on hazards is published by HSE, the representatives are entitled to carry out inspections before three months have elapsed, or by agreement.

116 The frequency of inspections will depend on the nature of the work. Inspections may be less often, for example if the work environment is low-risk, such as in an administrative office. But, if there are certain areas of a workplace or specific activities that are high-risk or changing rapidly, more frequent inspection may be justified, for example on a construction project.

Good practice

Inspecting the workplace with representatives

117 You and your representatives can plan a programme of inspections in advance, as this would satisfy the requirement to notify. You can do this at a health and safety committee meeting if you have one. This means both parties know and agree what inspections are happening, and where and when. Any changes to the planned inspections should then also be made by agreement.

118 You should also agree the number of representatives taking part in any one formal inspection. Bear in mind the nature of the inspection and circumstances in the workplace to judge what is suitable.

119 It is particularly important to plan inspections if there is more than one representative, because they can then co-ordinate their inspections to avoid unnecessary duplication.

120 It will help your relationship with the representatives if you inspect together. It shows that you value their contribution and want to work together. But it does not prevent union-appointed representatives from carrying out an independent inspection or having private discussions with colleagues.

121 If there is a health and safety officer or you have specialist advisers, then they should be available to give technical advice on health and safety matters that come up during an inspection.

122 For larger workplaces, it may not be practical to conduct a formal inspection of the entire workplace in a single session, or for a complete inspection to be done by the same representatives. You should consider doing inspections in more manageable units, for example by department. As part of a planned programme of inspections, you may also want to think about different groups of representatives conducting inspections in different parts of the workplace, either simultaneously or at different times, but they need to be completed before the next session of inspections are due.

Following-up after an inspection
123 After an inspection:

- explain the reasons for any follow-up action you decide to take to your representatives;
- let the representative who notified you of the inspection have the opportunity to inspect again so they can check if the issues raised got appropriate attention, and record their views; and
- share the follow-up action taken throughout the workplace and other relevant parts of the business, including the health and safety committee where there is one.

124 There may be times when action may not be appropriate, you may not be able to act within a reasonable period of time, or when the action you take is not acceptable to your health and safety representatives. It is advisable to explain the reasons for the action you have decided to take in writing to your representatives. You can even use the sample forms on the HSE website to do this.[8,9] You remain responsible for taking decisions about managing health and

safety, but by explaining the reasons for actions and being open with your representatives, you can show that you have considered what they had to say.

Health and safety committees: Setting them up and making them work

125 If two or more union-appointed health and safety representatives request in writing that you set up a health and safety committee, you must do so within three months of the request. Although there is no such requirement if you consult health and safety representatives elected by the workforce, it is good practice to set up a health and safety committee where:

- you have several health and safety representatives elected by employees; or
- you have to consult both union-appointed health and safety representatives and employee-elected representatives.

126 If you and your health and safety representatives want to set up a dedicated health and safety committee, it is useful to agree together:

- the principles of how it will function best so it is clear for all employees and members of the committee;
- who the members will be;
- what the committee will do;
- how you will make decisions and deal with disagreements; and
- what resources representatives will need as committee members.

Agree the principles
127 The best way to set out the basic rules and procedures of how the health and safety committee will work is to have a written constitution on what they will do to manage health, safety and welfare together. This should include its:

- purpose and objectives;
- membership;
- meeting arrangements; and
- arrangements for reporting the outcome of meetings to employees.

Case study

Springfield Fuels

Springfield Fuels, a nuclear fuel fabrication facility, ensures everyone on site is involved when making decisions about their employees' health and wellbeing. Their partnership approach has resulted in joint working groups, joint accident investigations, and several other effective initiatives because they recognise that everyone has a part to play in managing health and safety.

The challenge

With over 1400 employees and contractors on site, and health and safety issues ranging from stress to developing a strong behavioural safety culture, Springfield Fuels had to develop methods of involvement that tackled both technical and behavioural obstacles.

Getting the workforce on board

A behavioural safety programme, originally led by managers, has now been devolved to the shopfloor. Workers organise and present workshops on different safety issues for their colleagues to maintain focus and reaffirm commitment. They staged external events, like driving skills courses, which were specially designed to reinforce safety principles such as pre-job briefs, risk assessments, and peer checks. The target is for over 90% of employees to be involved in such a workshop every year. It is a culture that makes it easy for people to have their ideas adopted.

'At one time, this sort of initiative might have been met with resistance but we've found that this new safety culture has been widely accepted. It's very important that people don't feel they are being criticised or think that they will be disciplined if they have an accident at work. Our willingness to work together in partnership to overcome both technical and behavioural obstacles has been a key to our success.'
Derek McMillan, SFL's Site Behavioural Safety Co-ordinator

How is the workforce involved in the joint health and safety partnership?

- Springfield Fuels formed a joint working group made up of unions and non-union employee health and safety representatives, human resources, management and occupational health advisers. Their aim was to look at the impact of a new shiftworking system on workers' health and wellbeing. A questionnaire was produced by the group and sent to all shiftworkers, and this was backed up by good communication with them and members of the group. By involving the workers themselves, they came to a conclusion that satisfied everyone.
- Regular 'Safety in Partnership' meetings involve a cross-section of employees, including contractors. Participants are encouraged to bring along examples of good practice so they can be shared with the whole site.

- Health and safety representatives are actively involved in incident and accident investigations. Following all minor accidents, a small group of that section's workers look at what lessons can be learned using an accident awareness form. The form asks for views on causes and, if appropriate, remedial action. Any actions from this group are tracked by one of the Safety Improvement Teams in that area. Membership of these teams is open to anyone with an interest in local safety issues.
- Some workers have attended external workshops that train them to become 'workplace listeners' so they will pick up on the first signs of stress and steer people to help.

Benefits so far

20 November 2007 marked 285 days without a 'lost-time injury' – a huge milestone for Springfield Fuels' safety performance, and their best this century. They have also seen a significant increase in near-miss reporting on site. Local near-miss newsletters are produced and feedback is given on all near-miss incidents reported.

Keep improving

To mark this major milestone of 285 days without a 'lost-time injury', employees held a 'safety stand-down' day when they looked at local safety issues to avoid complacency and to refocus.

'The thing that sets us apart from the rest is our partnership approach and the involvement of everyone on site to ensure that health and safety remains our number one priority. This has given us the confidence to introduce initiatives such as 'workplace listeners'.

'Our approach is to involve everyone working in partnership so that all employees and contractors own, enforce and live behavioural health and safety 24/7. This provides us with a strong culture where everyone owns and is responsible for safety on site.'

128 Acas can provide more information about committee constitutions, including a checklist on their website (www.acas.org.uk).

129 The idea is to create the most effective arrangements for your business, and co-ordination between the work of the committee and the health and safety representatives on the committee.

Membership

130 There is no correct number of committee members because the circumstances will vary from business to business. Generally speaking, committee members can include:

- management representatives that have the authority to give proper consideration to views and recommendations;
- employee representatives, either appointed by a trade union, elected by your workforce, or a combination of both, who have knowledge of the work of those they represent;
- representatives of others in the workplace such as contractors; and
- co-opted workers and others. These are people who are included because of their specific competences such as the company doctor, health and safety adviser, and other specialists.

Good practice

131 A health and safety committee made up of employee representatives, union-appointed representatives, management, and health and safety professionals is an ideal way of showing your commitment to consulting your workers and jointly dealing with health and safety issues.

What will the health and safety committee do?

132 The general areas you must consult your workforce about are explained in paragraph 53. A committee meeting gives you the opportunity to discuss these matters with your employee representatives.

133 To ensure you cover all relevant issues, the committee should agree some standing items for the agenda and allow for other items to be added as necessary.

Consider standing items such as:

- statistics on accident records, ill health and sickness absence;
- accident investigations and subsequent action;
- inspections of the workplace by enforcing authorities, management or employee health and safety representatives;
- risk assessments;
- health and safety training;
- emergency procedures;
- changes in the workplace affecting the health, safety and welfare of employees; and
- adequacy of health and safety communications and publicity in the workplace.

Good practice

134 When considering statistics on accident and injury records, examine some information about minor injuries and incidents that you do not have to notify as well as the ones you do have to report. This can be valuable in drawing attention to issues across your business.

135 If the health and safety committee is discussing accidents, the point is to stop them happening again, not to give blame. Committees should:

- look at the facts of the case in an impartial way;
- consider what sorts of precautions might be taken;
- make appropriate recommendations; and
- monitor progress with implementing health and safety interventions.

Good practice

136 Where possible, plan a series of committee meetings in advance but remain flexible to address important matters as they come up.

137 All committee members should have a personal copy of the planned meeting dates, and they should be available where all employees can see them, for instance on notice boards or intranet pages.

138 It is important that committee meetings are not postponed or cancelled unless there are exceptional circumstances, or members have agreed to it. If the meeting is cancelled, another agreed date should be arranged as soon as possible otherwise issues will not be addressed and the work of the committee, plus the value of health and safety, is undermined.

139 To be effective, health and safety committees should address strategic issues affecting the workforce or groups within the workforce, and allow day-to-day health and safety matters to be resolved at a local level.

Making decisions and dealing with disagreements

140 The committee can be powerful in making improvements in the workplace. When considering issues, the committee should:

- discuss if action is needed;
- make recommendations for agreed action;
- record the discussion and actions in the minutes of the meeting (which should be accessible to the whole workforce); and
- follow up the actions, then review them at a later date.

141 A safety committee requires good communication between you and the committee members, and between the committee members and employees.

Good practice

142 To help reach agreements on recommendations remember:

- all members are committed to the committee's aims and all views should be considered with respect. Both management and employee representatives will have expertise and knowledge to help make suitable recommendations;
- the committee chair can be effective in summarising points and helping the committee to come to reasonable recommendations;
- management representatives on the committee should have the authority to consider recommendations. Ultimately, the employer is responsible for managing

health and safety, so you must decide how you choose to address the committee's feedback.

143 If committee members cannot agree on solutions:

- recommend a range of possible options, not just a preferred approach, which management can consider;
- explain how and why decisions are reached to demonstrate how views have been considered; or
- review the situation at a later date.

144 If there are disagreements that cannot be resolved, consider following the procedures for employment relations disputes or contact Acas for advice (see 'Sources of advice' for contact details).

What resources will employee representatives need as committee members?

145 It is good practice to provide both health and safety representatives appointed by trade unions and those elected by your employees with the same resources, although you are only required to do this for the former. Health and safety representatives need to have:

- time to prepare for meetings as management representatives would;
- access to the same information for the purposes of the discussion at the meetings; and
- training that is reasonable in the circumstances to allow them to perform their role, which includes attending health and safety committee meetings for union-appointed representatives. Training for representatives can help them to contribute equally to the committee's aims and purpose.

146 Being a member of the health and safety committee is part of a person's role as a health and safety representative, so they should not suffer a loss of pay when they attend meetings or carry out other activities on behalf of the committee.

UCATT North-West

The Union of Construction Allied Trades and Technicians (UCATT) has a long-standing policy of partnership and co-operation with employers and employees on health and safety matters. Although the union firmly believes in the value of health and safety committees, it warns that many organisations jump too quickly when putting together such committees without the appropriate preparation.

The challenge
Billy Baldwin, North-West (Regional) Safety Adviser for UCATT, advised joint health and safety committees on two major construction projects with Bovis/Manchester Joint Hospitals Project and Media City in Salford, to ensure they were well put together and ran as effectively as possible.

Where to start?
'Health and safety committees are important but they are not sufficient on their own. Their members must be equipped with the knowledge, training and experience that will allow them to be truly effective.

'It was important to start the process as a forum for operatives before it evolved into a full health and safety committee because many participants needed to gain certain skills.

'The key is to lay solid foundations for an effective committee. Participants will be from all backgrounds and levels. The meeting can easily descend into chaos if it is not kept in focus.'

Membership
Potential members of the forum were identified through various channels, eg operatives who had raised issues on site, union health and safety representatives, and health and safety advisers. Non-union members were also invited to join, as all employees have a role to play in joint problem solving.

Towards joint working
Steered by Billy Baldwin, they initially agreed a constitution for the forum with clear objectives, membership requirements, general functions and frequency of meetings.

'In my experience, operatives do not generally have the knowledge and training needed to identify site-wide issues and usually want to concentrate on issues directly affecting them, such as the cleanliness of welfare facilities etc.

'An effective committee member will usually need training in the procedures of a meeting. They also need experience and this can be provided by the initial forum.

'A common mistake is for organisations to form a health and safety committee and then invite workers to join it and turn up with a list of problems for the employer to solve. But it doesn't work that way – you should never say to an employer "You've got a problem". It should be "We've got a problem and here are some potential solutions we can look at".'

Key tips for an effective joint health and safety committee
- Don't just duplicate another organisation's health and safety structure. It won't work.
- Properly training health and safety representatives (whether they are union members or not) is vital. Make sure they are properly empowered by full training and support.
- When people bring issues to the health and safety committee, it is vital they are given a fair hearing and none should be dismissed outright. If something is unsuitable, a full explanation should be given. If there are any actions resulting from a meeting, names should be clearly assigned.
- To raise their profile, health and safety representatives can be issued with different coloured high-visibility vests or other clearly defined work clothes.
- It is vital to develop the mindset that every worker is valued and has the chance to contribute to health and safety.

Successful outcomes
A key role for a health and safety committee is to allow time for a 'good practice session' in which any issues that health and safety representatives have helped resolve are discussed and noted.

Examples of this, from one meeting at Manchester's Royal Infirmary, include:

- a health and safety representative who removed the risk to welders using equipment which caused exhaust fumes by arranging for the equipment to be moved to an area with suitable ventilation;
- a health and safety representative saw some operatives working on a platform without proper edge protection. He pointed out to them that it was a dangerous situation but was ignored. He then told the site safety adviser, who immediately suspended the work.

Another example of the committee's work during the Bovis/Manchester Joint Hospitals project is the formalising of the procedure for 'stopping work due to imminent danger'.

The stop work procedure, which was put onto a pocket card and issued to all workers, contains the simple reminder that if any operative feels they are in imminent danger, they must stop work immediately and report the circumstances to their supervisor, who must then assess the situation. If the operative is still concerned, they have the right to refer the matter to a project manager or safety adviser.

There was some concern that operatives may use this procedure unnecessarily but what actually happened was that it encouraged supervisors to resolve issues after the first contact rather than having to follow the procedure to its final outcome.

Real benefits and continuous improvement
The Bovis project has an above-average safety record and other north-west projects are recognising this success and following their example.

Get it right: Keep improving

147 This section is about how to make sure your arrangements for workforce involvement are effective as possible and covers how you can keep improving by:

- monitoring performance;
- reviewing progress; and
- knowing what to do when things become challenging.

148 Once you have been consulting and involving your employees for a while and given each other time to adjust to the processes you have set in place, you should start thinking about how to keep improving over time. Realistically, there are likely to be some things that work really well, others that could work better, and some things that need to be approached in a different way. This is not something to worry about as things are rarely perfect at the first attempt. Even when some things are working well, changes over time may mean they do not remain effective.

149 For effective employee engagement, you need to keep monitoring performance and reviewing progress **regularly** with your workforce and employee representatives. It allows you to continue improving the way you work together to enhance health and safety. You can also explore what others in your industry or similar businesses do to find out what works and share experiences of successful measures.

150 If you have had success with worker involvement tackling safety issues then consider other issues. Engagement with your workforce is a powerful way to tackle musculoskeletal problems like back pain, work-related stress and other health problems where psychological and social factors contribute.

Monitor performance

151 To keep an eye on how involvement with your employees is working, you should:

- Check how supportive management are by asking employees and their representatives if they have been encouraged to get involved and been given time to participate.
- Check that employees know who their representatives are and whether they have been asked for their views about health and safety matters.
- Look into organisational arrangements for involving the workforce in health and safety and whether they have changed to allow employees greater opportunity to be involved in consultation. For example, have training arrangements improved, or do representatives have their roles noted on their performance appraisals?
- Collect information on health and safety issues and ideas for addressing them that have been raised as a result of employee involvement to see if there have been improvements in how they are managed.
- Think about other measures beyond health and safety because involving your workforce in health and safety could result in additional benefits, for example in productivity, as things improve.

152 When you monitor performance, ask yourself if:

- what you find is acceptable or if you need to do something more;
- you need to address a matter further, how you will do this and what your employees think;
- there are any lessons to learn.

Good practice

153 You will be doing well if you can show:

- employees are aware of their health and safety representative and they communicate with each other;
- co-operation between managers and employees so that there are the resources to release people for meetings and training;
- a health and safety committee that deals with strategic matters balanced with everyday problems that are resolved as they happen;
- good communication with and through the workforce so that messages are delivered clearly and decisions are explained;
- competence is built through training and information sharing so new skills can be learned as there are changes;
- joint problem solving, where employees participate as equals to resolve issues;
- joint inspections and monitoring of health and safety performance, risk control systems, and progress with plans.

Review progress

154 As well as thinking about how well consultation with your workforce is going, check how far you have progressed and consider where there is room for improvement. The review checklist can help you assess how close you are to moving towards full employee involvement and joint problem solving.

155 The statements are essentially goals to aim for, so you can consider whether your arrangements are helping you to achieve those objectives, and where they are not, revisit areas to improve involvement. Not everything on the list will apply to all businesses. There may be other factors not covered that are more relevant for you but the statements are general guidelines to help you see how you are doing.

Review checklist

✓ Gain commitment and action from senior management to involve employees and their representatives in good time about matters affecting their health and safety.

✓ Fully involve employees and health and safety representatives in discussions about health and safety matters affecting them, and encourage the workforce to generate ideas for health and safety initiatives.

✓ Train managers, employees and health and safety representatives together in health and safety matters to enable shared understanding and greater co-operation.

✓ Use a range of methods to consult and involve employees to appropriately and effectively take into account the needs of different groups of the workforce who are affected by health and safety measures.

✓ Give health and safety representatives access to the facilities and training they reasonably need to perform their role.

✓ Ensure the health and safety committee members are equal partners, working together to address strategic matters, and day-to-day matters are resolved elsewhere.

✓ Involve health and safety representatives in joint accident investigations, workplace inspections and risk assessments.

✓ Explain the reasons behind management decisions so the workforce can understand how their views have been considered in making decisions about managing their health and safety.

✓ Build on the success of workforce involvement in some issues by engaging employees in discussions of health and safety issues that can be more challenging.

✓ Review progress with involving the workforce in health and safety and update consultation processes so they are current and effective.

Case study

University of Leeds

The University of Leeds launched a revitalisation programme in partnership with campus trade unions to bring about significant and lasting improvements to health and safety performance.

The challenge

Around one in ten university staff reported an accident at work, and the university had also received two improvement notices from HSE in the last three years. Managers and staff recognised that there was room for improvement.

With jobs ranging from laboratory experiments to office administration, and from fieldwork in the Arctic to serving lunch in the canteen, the university's 8000 staff have a very diverse range of health and safety issues and are spread across 98 acres of campus. The key challenge was raising awareness of health and safety issues and getting everyone involved.

Getting the workforce on board

The university launched a revitalisation programme with the three campus trade unions where both unions and management are equal partners in achieving health and safety standards and resolving issues. A declaration that health and safety is one of the university's top priorities is at the heart of the partnership.

'The revitalising agreement allowed the university and the campus trade unions to start again and build from scratch a new working
relationship and develop a refocused approach to health and safety. This will in time lead to a culture change across campus and has already led to an official partnership which is the first of its kind.'
Nick Creighton, Branch Health and Safety Officer, on behalf of the Unison University of Leeds Branch

Raising awareness

'It was essential to make sure that everyone understood their own health and safety responsibilities and knew what could happen if these weren't taken seriously. This required a change in both attitudes and behaviour.'
Gary Tideswell, Director of Wellbeing, Safety and Health

A DVD was made using contributions from staff across the university. It highlighted what can happen if health and safety is not taken seriously, and also gave examples of best practice. Every member of staff watched the film, was then encouraged to talk about local issues and priorities, and received information on individual health and safety responsibilities.

' . . . the DVD and briefings created an opportunity for dialogue by using real case studies from our campus and giving people the chance to ask questions and discuss local issues.'
Gary Tideswell, Director of Wellbeing, Safety and Health

How is the workforce involved?

- A health and safety committee was formed with representatives from all areas of the university, including health and safety representatives appointed by
the trade unions. It works to clear terms of reference and monitors arrangements for managing health and safety, considers incident reports, and makes recommendations for improvements.
- As part of the revitalisation agreement, a sub-group of the main committee was formed to include trade unions and meets between the main meetings at short notice, if necessary, to consider urgent health and safety matters. It also provides a sounding board for developing new or revised policies.

Benefits so far

- There has been a notable change in the awareness and attitudes of staff – they understand the issues more now and engage more readily.
- The staff now have clearer, more accessible information and they are more aware of their own health and safety responsibilities.
- Although it is too early to measure a reduction in accidents, the university is confident that their accident reporting system now provides a more accurate picture.

Keep improving

'We need to bring about a permanent shift in health and safety culture. We should not underestimate the challenge of achieving this, but I am confident that by working together we will succeed. I look forward to the day when our university is a flagship for health and safety, with others looking to us to see how it should be done.'
Professor Michael Arthur, Vice-Chancellor

When things become challenging

156 There may be times when:

- you and your employees or their representatives disagree about health and safety issues; or
- health and safety issues are sometimes used as a substitute for other workplace relations issues because consulting and involving your employees are linked to wider employment relations.

157 You should have agreed processes in place to deal with disagreements, and wherever possible you should use these procedures to resolve any issues. If you and your employees need more help to reach agreement you can:

- involve regional or national trade union officials if you recognise trade unions;
- approach your trade association for advice if you belong to one; and
- contact Acas.

158 Health and safety inspectors can only advise on health and safety matters. They cannot arbitrate in workplace disputes between you and your employees.

Good practice

159 If things do become challenging, seek help and assistance as soon as possible to address the issues. Managers, employees and their representatives are equally responsible for building a relationship of trust, respect, co-operation and joint problem solving. Disputes and disagreements can damage everyone's efforts towards developing a good health and safety culture.

References and further reading

References

1   *Consulting workers on health and safety. Safety Representatives and Safety Committees Regulations 1977 (as amended) and Health and Safety (Consultation with Employees) Regulations 1996 (as amended). Approved Codes of Practice and guidance* L146 HSE Books ISBN 978 0 7176 6311 8

2   *Consulting employees on health and safety: A brief guide to the law* INDG232(rev1) HSE Books 2008 (single copy free or priced packs of 15 ISBN 978 0 7176 6312 5) www.hse.gov.uk/pubns/indg232.pdf

3   *A guide to the Offshore Installations (Safety Representatives and Safety Committees) Regulations 1989. Guidance on Regulations* L110 (Second edition) HSE Books 1998 ISBN 978 0 7176 1549 0

4   *Play your part! How offshore workers can improve health and safety* Booklet INDG421 HSE Books 2008 (single copy free or priced packs of 10 ISBN 978 0 7176 6286 9) www.hse.gov.uk/pubns/indg421.pdf

5   *Enforcement policy statement* HSE41 HSE Books 2008 (www.hse.gov.uk/enforce)

6   *Management of health and safety at work. Management of Health and Safety at Work Regulations 1999. Approved Code of Practice and guidance* L21 (Second edition) HSE Books 2000 ISBN 978 0 7176 2488 1

7   *Employee communications and consultation* Acas 2005 www.acas.org.uk

8   Form F2534 www.hse.gov.uk/forms/incident/f2533.pdf

9   Form F2533 www.hse.gov.uk/forms/incident/f2534.pdf

Further reading

Leading health and safety at work: Leadership actions for directors and board members Leaflet INDG417 HSE Books 2007 (single copy free or priced packs of 5 ISBN 978 0 7176 6267 8) www.hse.gov.uk/pubns/indg417.pdf

Worker involvement website: www.hse.gov.uk/involvement

Further information

HSE priced and free publications are available by mail order from HSE Books, PO Box 1999, Sudbury, Suffolk CO10 2WA Tel: 01787 881165 Fax: 01787 313995 Website: www.hsebooks.co.uk (HSE priced publications are also available from bookshops and free leaflets can be downloaded from HSE's website: www.hse.gov.uk.)

Sources of advice

HSE Infoline

For information about health and safety ring HSE's Infoline Tel: 0845 345 0055 Fax: 0845 408 9566 Textphone: 0845 408 9577 e-mail: hse.infoline@natbrit.com or write to HSE Information Services, Caerphilly Business Park, Caerphilly CF83 3GG.

Acas

The Acas Helpline is the place to go for both employers and employees who are involved in an employment dispute or are seeking information on employment rights and rules. The Helpline provides clear, confidential, independent and impartial advice to help the caller resolve issues in the workplace.

Helpline numbers:
Monday to Friday 08:00-18:00 Tel: 08457 47 47 47 or for Minicom users Tel: 08456 06 16 00

Website: www.acas.org.uk

Printed and published by the Health and Safety Executive   C100   10/08